50 Quick Ways to   the

By Mike Gershon

Text Copyright © 2017 Mike Gershon

All Rights Reserved

About the Author

Mike Gershon is an expert educationalist who works throughout the UK and abroad helping teachers to develop their practice. His knowledge of teaching and learning is rooted in the practicalities of the classroom and his online teaching tools have been viewed and downloaded more than 3.5 million times, making them some of the most popular of all time.

He is the author of over 80 books and guides covering different areas of teaching and learning. Some of Mike's bestsellers include books on assessment for learning, questioning, differentiation and outstanding teaching, as well as Growth Mindsets. You can train online with Mike, from anywhere in the world, at www.tes.com/institute/cpd-courses-teachers.

You can also find out more at www.mikegershon.com and www.gershongrowthmindsets.com, including about Mike's inspirational in-school training and student workshops.

Training and Consultancy

Mike offers a range of training and consultancy services covering all areas of teaching and learning, raising achievement and classroom practice. He runs inspiring and engaging INSET in primary schools, secondary schools and colleges. Examples of recent training events include:

- Growth Mindsets: Theory and Practice – William Bellamy Primary School, Dagenham
- Creating a Challenge Culture: Stretch and Challenge Reimagined – Manchester College
- Rethinking Differentiation – The British School of Brussels

To find out more, visit www.mikegershon.com or www.gershongrowthmindsets.com or get in touch via mike@mikegershon.com

Other Works from the Same Author

Available to buy now on Amazon:

How to Develop Growth Mindsets in the Classroom: The Complete Guide

How to use Differentiation in the Classroom: The Complete Guide

How to use Assessment for Learning in the Classroom: The Complete Guide

How to use Bloom's Taxonomy in the Classroom: The Complete Guide

How to use Questioning in the Classroom: The Complete Guide

How to use Discussion in the Classroom: The Complete Guide

How to Manage Behaviour in the Classroom: The Complete Guide

How to Teach EAL Students in the Classroom: The Complete Guide

How to be an Outstanding Trainee Teacher: The Complete Guide

More Secondary Starters and Plenaries

Secondary Starters and Plenaries: History

Teach Now! History: Becoming a Great History Teacher

The Growth Mindset Pocketbook (with Professor Barry Hymer)

The Exams, Tests and Revision Pocketbook

Also available to buy now on Amazon, the entire 'Quick 50' Series:

50 Quick Ways to Get Past 'I Don't Know'

50 Quick Ways to Start Your Lessons with a Bang!

50 Quick Ways to Improve Literacy Across the Curriculum

50 Quick Ways to Improve Feedback and Marking

50 Quick Ways to Use Scaffolding and Modelling

50 Quick Ways to Stretch and Challenge More-Able Students

50 Quick Ways to Create Independent Learners

50 Quick Ways to go from Good to Outstanding

50 Quick Ways to Support Less-Able Learners

50 Quick and Brilliant Teaching Ideas

50 Quick and Brilliant Teaching Techniques

50 Quick and Easy Lesson Activities

50 Quick Ways to Help Your Students Secure A and B Grades at GCSE

50 Quick Ways to Help Your Students Think, Learn, and Use Their Brains Brilliantly

50 Quick Ways to Motivate and Engage Your Students

50 Quick Ways to Outstanding Teaching

50 Quick Ways to Perfect Behaviour Management

50 Quick and Brilliant Teaching Games

50 Quick and Easy Ways Leaders Can Prepare for Ofsted

50 Quick and Easy Ways to Outstanding Group Work

50 Quick and Easy Ways to Prepare for Ofsted

About the Series

The 'Quick 50' series was born out of a desire to provide teachers with practical, tried and tested ideas, activities, strategies and techniques which would help them to teach brilliant lessons, raise achievement and engage and inspire their students.

Every title in the series distils great teaching wisdom into fifty bite-sized chunks. These are easy to digest and easy to apply – perfect for the busy teacher who wants to develop their practice and support their students.

Acknowledgements

My thanks to all the staff and students I have worked with past and present, particularly those at Pimlico Academy and King Edward VI School, Bury St Edmunds. Thanks also to the teachers and teaching assistants who have attended my training sessions and who always offer great insights into what works in the classroom. Finally, thanks to Gordon at Kall Kwik for his design work.

Table of Contents

Introduction 13

Speaking, Listening, Reading and Writing 15

Paired Discussion 17

Group Discussion 19

Triads 21

Stimulus Discussion 23

Structuring Discussion 25

Discussion Preceding Writing 27

Discussion of Questions 28

Interviewing 30

Conceptual Discussion 32

Capturing Discussion 34

Verbalising Thoughts 36

Refining and Editing Ideas 38

Verbal Rehearsal 40

Practising New Words 42

Word Banks 44

Sentence Starters 46

Model Sentences 48

Genre Conventions 50

Writing Models 52

Structure Guidelines 53

Defining Purpose..55

Defining Success 57

Exemplar Work 59

Annotated Exemplar Work 61

Goldfish Bowl 63

Narrated Marking 65

Modelling Thought Processes 66

Six Ways to Start a Sentence..68

Defining the Audience 69

Keyword Quotas 71

Keyword Mindmaps 73

Verbal Feedback 75

Editing Techniques...77

Literacy Checklists 79

Self-Assessment 81

Focussed Practice...83

Active Repetition with Targets.......................................85

Reading Techniques 86

Reading for Questions..88

Reading and Note-Taking...90

Decoding Texts – Tips and Techniques 92

Dictionaries and Thesauruses 94

- Dividing Up Writing 96
- Planning Techniques 98
- Thinking Maps 100
- Whole-Class Bounce 102
- Distancing 104
- Modelling Great Literacy 106
- Websites and Resources 108
- A Brief Request 110

Introduction

Welcome to 50 Quick Ways to Improve Literacy Across the Curriculum. This book is intended for any teacher who wants to help students develop their speaking, listening, reading and writing. You might be responsible for literacy across your school, or you might be a subject or year group teacher who understands the vital role literacy plays in any child's development.

Whatever brings you to this book, you will find a wide range of practical strategies, activities and techniques in the pages which follow. My aim has been to create a pocketbook of ideas any teacher can take and apply to their own teaching – or disseminate through school to support others in their efforts to improve literacy.

As you read on, you might start to wonder whether there is too much to do all at once. Well, yes there is! Fifty different things is far too many to implement in one go. I would suggest reading the book through in full to begin with and then pulling out a handful of ideas which really chime with you and which you feel will be of particular benefit to your students. These can then be your starting point for improving learners' literacy.

As time goes on, you can come back to the book and remind yourself of other ideas, which you can use to further develop your practice. Taking this approach means that, over a sustained period, your ability to develop learners' literacy will grow and grow.

The final point to make is that in all the entries which follow there is room for modification and adaptation. Everyone has their own teaching style and a particular set of learners with whom they work. So don't be afraid to tweak some of the ideas as you see fit – or to engage in a bit of trial and error, until you get them working in the way you want.

Speaking, Listening, Reading and Writing

01 Four elements make up literacy: speaking, listening, reading and writing. When we talk about literacy across the curriculum, we are talking about students' ability to both render their thoughts through words (speaking, writing) and access the thoughts of others (listening, reading).

Speaking and listening may be considered natural functions of the human body, whereas writing and reading are a result of cultural developments within human societies. Many purely oral societies, communities and groups have existed – a few still do. But there has been no society in which reading and writing existed prior to and independently of speaking and listening.

This illustrates a key point regarding the wider nature of literacy: writing is a technology which is learned in a different way from speech. Speech, I would argue, is not a technology. In the context of this book I am taking technology to mean a human invention which expands the capacity of what it is possible for us to achieve with our minds and bodies alone. Just as a chisel is a technology – a tool – so too, I am arguing, is writing.

In what follows you will therefore see an underlying message about the benefits of using speaking and listening as a means through which to develop and improve reading and writing, as well as students' thinking more generally.

This stems from the premise, inherent in what I have just written, that students will nearly always be better speakers than writers. We can make use of this – to our and to their advantage.

Paired Discussion

02 Paired discussion allows students to articulate their thoughts in a safe space, prior to sharing those thoughts or doing something with them. There are at least three further benefits. First, the student has a chance to edit and refine their thoughts. Second, they can hear the thoughts of others, which often leads to reflection on and development of their own thinking. Third, if the teacher wants to know what students think, they can find out by asking:

'What came up in your discussion?'

'What did you and your partner talk about?'

'Can you summarise your discussion for me?'

In each case, the student is asked to explain what has already been said. This lowers the risk attached to answering the teacher's question. Which, in turn, increases the likelihood a response will be shared.

Paired discussion can be used in a range of settings:

- When a teacher has posed a question to the whole class.

- When a task has been set ('Discuss with your partner how you will get started)

- Half-way through a task ('30 seconds – discuss with your partner where you are at and what you're going to do next)

- In response to a stimulus

- Prior to a piece of writing

For me, it is a go to technique throughout lessons. A quick and easy way to promote active engagement, refinement of ideas and articulation of thinking.

Group Discussion

03 By group discussion I mean any discussion involving 3 or more students.

The biggest risk with group discussion is that students do not focus their efforts on the task in hand, or that some students become passengers.

Avoid this by keeping group sizes small (3 or 4 is ideal) and by carefully structuring the discussion. Here are five examples of how to do it:

- Give groups a series of three related questions they must discuss in turn.

- Set a goal and a time limit. For example: 'In three minutes I want you to decide which of the quotes is most relevant and to identify two key reasons which support your choice.'

- Provide a question along with a set of caveats. For example: 'Why does strategy matter in team sports?' Discuss in your groups. Caveat one: Each member of the group must use a different team sport to make their points. Caveat two: You must first define what strategy means.

- Give each group a different question to discuss. Explain that you will pick groups at random to share their thoughts.

- Appoint a scribe in each group to take notes. This can be further structured through the provision of a pro-forma.

A final thought. As the students you teach get used to your expectations regarding group discussion, so the necessity of having a high degree of teacher-led structuring is likely to disappear.

Triads

04 Triads is a specific form of group discussion. Its use is advocated here for two reasons. First, the wider benefits of practising speaking and listening and using this as a way into further thinking, writing and reading. Second, the structure of the activity differs sufficiently from paired and group discussion to warrant an additional entry. It works as follows:

Students work in groups of three. In each group students are labelled A, B and C. The teacher presents a discussion question. Students A and B discuss this while Student C observes. After sufficient time has passed, the teacher stops the activity and asks Student C to feed back to their peers. The activity is repeated three times with different combinations and questions:

1: Students A and B discuss question 1. Student C observes and feeds back.

2: Students A and C discuss question 2. Student B observes and feeds back.

3: Students B and C discuss question 3. Student A observes and feeds back.

You can support the third student's observation by specifying things you want them to look out for. You can also provide observation sheets if you feel it necessary. Finally, you might like to model the activity in full to help students understand how it works. If you choose to do this, you can also talk through the benefits as you go – both in terms of speaking and listening and in terms of receiving critical feedback.

Stimulus Discussion

05 In a stimulus discussion the teacher provides something intended to stimulate student thinking. This differs from discussions framed by a question, or series of questions.

In a stimulus discussion, a two-step process is at work. First the teacher shares the stimulus with students, then they provide a few ideas to underpin the discussion. Here is an example:

In a Food Technology lesson the teacher brings in a plastic bag filled with individually wrapped sweets. Students sit in pairs and each receive three sweets. They are expressly forbidden from eating them!

The teacher explains that the sweets are a stimulus for discussion and gives students a couple of minutes to examine them, talk about them and consider where the activity might be going next.

Then, they provide a clutch of questions intended to gently shepherd the discussion, while still giving students scope to explore the stimulus and think creatively:

- Why don't all sweets look the same?

- What is the point in packaging individual sweets – why not just put them all in a box or a bag?

- What does it mean to 'eat with your eyes?'

- Is one of your sweets better than the others? Why?

- How much design is involved in food technology?

Notice how a stimulus, when artfully chosen, facilitates a discussion which is harder to achieve if questions alone are used.

Structuring Discussion

06 Here are a few more strategies and techniques you can use to structure discussions:

- Present students with a list of questions and invite them to select the ones they most want to discuss. This creates a sense of agency and motivation.

- Ask students to discuss the ways in which an activity could be attempted. You can provide a range of possible options or leave it up to your students to devise different methods. This is a good precursor to an activity with which students are unfamiliar.

- Share a key question with the class, then break this down into three sub-questions. Divide the class into three and assign one sub-question to each third. Give time for discussion and then invite students from each third to summarise their thinking for the rest of the class.

- Students work in pairs. The teacher displays a question on the board, along with a list of interrogative sub-questions. They ask pairs to define themselves as A and B. Student B then uses the list of sub-questions to interrogate the thinking of Student A.

- Provide students with a questioning crib sheet they can use to construct questions during a discussion. For example, a laminated sheet containing a selection of keywords covering each different level of Bloom's Taxonomy.

Discussion Preceding Writing

07 Imagine you want to write something. Instead of immediately getting started you ring up your friend and chat to them about your ideas. Then, you put the phone down and begin to write.

What has happened?

Well, during the course of your discussion you have given yourself an opportunity to articulate, refine and edit your thoughts. This makes it easier to start writing. The cognitive work has been divided, giving you the opportunity to focus exclusively on the act of writing, rather than having to divide your attention between what you want to say and how you will say it (inscribe it through the written word).

The same principle is at work when we use discussion to precede writing in the classroom. We give students an opportunity to articulate, refine and edit their thoughts before focussing their attention of the process of turning these into written words.

You can use any and all of the discussion techniques we have looked at thus far as a means to do this. For example, a geography lesson might see students discussing various aspects of migration before going on to write an extended answer about the relative costs and benefits of migration to a local economy.

Discussion of Questions

08 Questions are perhaps the primary mode of communication between teachers and students. We ask questions throughout the school day – and we also use written questions to structure activities and student thinking.

Discussion of questions sees us doing two things. First, making it clear to students that such a process is desirable. Second, providing a space, and possibly a structure, through which it can happen. Here is an example:

In a maths classroom the teacher is using the following question as the basis for the lesson: 'Can we predict random events?'

They intend to use this to help students think about probability and the law of large numbers. They begin the lesson by introducing the question, explaining a little about it and then providing space for discussion. They structure the discussion with the following sub-questions:

- What makes something random?

- How might we define an 'event' in maths?

- Is prediction the same as probability? Are they related? Are they different?

What you will note is that the process is designed to help students better understand the question, and thus the basis of the lesson, and to enhance their mathematical literacy. That is, their ability to invoke and use words relevant to the mathematics they are going to be doing.

Interviewing

09 Here is a simple speaking and listening activity you can use in almost any lesson. It helps students practice articulating and refining their thoughts, and also gives them access to other people's ideas. It works as follows:

Display a slide on the board with the following information:

'Your task is to interview at least three members of the class. You must find out what their thoughts are and be ready to compare these thoughts to your own.'

That is the basis of the activity. Students get up, move around the room and take it in turns to interview each other. The process gives plenty of opportunities for verbal rehearsal. This makes it a great precursor to written or practical work in which students implement their ideas.

Here is an example of how the activity might play out in a specific context:

'Your task is to interview at least three members of the class. You must find out what their thoughts are on the assassination of JFK and be ready to compare these thoughts to your own.

Use the following questions to structure your interview:

- What were the most significant short-term impacts of the assassination?

- How have interpretations of JFK's legacy changed over time?

- Did the assassination fundamentally alter the course of US history?'

Conceptual Discussion

10 Concepts play an integral role in all areas of the curriculum. They are the ideas which underpin our thinking. Sometimes they recur across subjects, sometimes they are specific to a subject. An example of the former is loss, a concept which means different things in English, physical education and business studies. An example of the latter is superconductivity, which would rarely be encountered outside a science classroom.

Conceptual discussion sees the teacher focussing students' speaking and listening on concepts relevant to the unit of work. The aim is to help students better understand these concepts by getting them to practice using them.

In short, a conceptual discussion is akin to any other type of discussion, only here it is a concept which is the subject of conversation. Examples include:

- A discussion in a maths lesson looking at the meaning of chance.

- A discussion in a literacy lesson focussing on the meaning of persuasion.

- A discussion in a history lesson examining the meaning of causality.

- A discussion in an art lesson exploring the meaning of taste.

- A discussion in a computing lesson analysing the meaning of logic.

Note how, in each case, the purpose of the discussion is to help students develop a better understanding of the concept (and by better I mean more nuanced) at the same time as they improve their ability to use the concept – in speech, in writing and, in some cases, in practical terms.

Capturing Discussion

11 Sometimes it can be beneficial to capture discussion, or the results of a discussion. This might be for administrative reasons (such as to show progress or demonstrate learning), cognitive reasons (to act as an aid to working memory), or learning reasons (to allow students to reflect at a later date).

Here are a range of ways through which you can capture the discussions your students have:

- Appoint a scribe who makes notes on what is said. Group scribes and whole-class scribes can be used. One option is to use different colours to indicate who said what.

- Use a device such as a mobile phone to make an audio recording of a discussion. Some software and apps allow you to cut, paste, edit and refine audio files.

- Provide students with a pro-forma they can use to make notes while they discuss. This can be fairly loose in design or highly prescriptive, depending on the students you are working with and what you want to achieve.

- At the end of the discussion, give students three minutes in which to make a brief written summary of what was discussed. You can scaffold this by suggesting particular areas they might like to focus on or by providing three stock questions such as: What did you discuss? What were the main themes? What do you feel was most relevant?

- Give students mini-whiteboards and ask them to make notes on these while they are discussing. At the end of the discussion, invite students to take photos of what they have written using their smartphones.

Verbalising Thoughts

12 Verbalising thoughts means taking what is inside our head and framing it in language which we then externalise through speech. This sees us using language as a bridge between minds. I think certain thoughts, I frame those in a linguistic structure I believe you will be able to understand, and I verbalise this through speech, turning it into something external which you, through hearing, can access, process and, I hope, comprehend.

Note what is inherent here.

The verbalisation of thought requires prior processes to give rise to that verbalisation. These processes might be distinct from the act of speaking – such as when a child sits and thinks before answering your question. Or, they might occur almost simultaneously – such as when a child responds instantly to something you say.

In either case, there remains a sense that the process of forming and then verbalising our thinking through speech provides us with a means through which to better understand what it is we do think. In addition, on hearing ourselves speak we are then in a position to reflect on what we have said. This further aids literacy development as we are confronted by questions such as: Do I actually agree with what I'm saying? Could I have said that differently? Do I still think what I just said?

All of which highlights the benefit of finding ways to help students verbalise their thoughts. For more on which, see the next entry.

Refining and Editing Ideas

13 Speech allows us to refine and edit our ideas. Verbalising thoughts is the first step. This lays the foundations. If we don't verbalise our thoughts, they are not as easy to refine and edit.

Here are some techniques you can use to help students verbalise their thoughts:

- **Allow wait time.** Ask a question, and then wait. Students need time to think. Don't expect them to verbalise their thoughts immediately. Give them space. Maybe even draw attention to what you are doing by saying something like: '30 seconds of silent thinking, then tell me what you think.'

- **Provide options.** If a student is struggling to verbalise their thoughts, present a set of options and ask them to select the one which most closely matches what they think. This gives them an opening; a way to start talking about their ideas.

- **Model your own thinking.** Show students what the process of verbalising thoughts looks like in this particular setting by modelling your own thinking. They can then imitate your model before going on to think for themselves.

- **Provide a sentence model to use.** For example: '30 seconds of silent thinking, then tell me your thoughts by using a sentence that starts with 'If...' and goes onto 'then...' (e.g. 'If Mary really did like Peter, then she wouldn't have pushed him over').

- **Call on images or objects.** If a child is struggling to articulate their thoughts, images and objects can act as a stimulus to help them get across the initial meaning of their ideas. You and they can use the image/object as a shared point of reference. From here it becomes easier to help the child say what they want to say.

Verbal Rehearsal

14 Verbal rehearsal is any situation in which students practise speaking their ideas on a number of occasions. They verbally rehearse their thinking, improving their understanding and retention of it in the process.

Verbal rehearsal is inherent in all discussion activities. You can also plan for lesson situations in which rehearsal is the primary focus. Here are some examples of how to do it:

- Ask students to write down their thoughts, or to produce a short piece of written work. They then move around the classroom and speak this aloud to a number of their peers.

- Divide the class into pairs. Present a question for pairs to discuss. After thirty seconds, invite students to split up and form new pairs. Indicate that the new pairs should discuss the same question. Repeat four or five times.

- Ask a student to talk you through their thinking. Then ask them to do it again, but this time to use fewer words. Finally, ask the student to talk you through their thinking using only three sentences.

- Divide the class in half. One half are speakers, the other half are listeners. Ask the speakers to find a listener and to tell them their thoughts on the topic, then to move on and repeat the process to a second, third and fourth listener. When the time is up, ask the class to swap roles and repeat a second time so that every student has a chance to engage in verbal rehearsal.

Practising New Words

15 As we practice new words, so they become more familiar to us. As we practice, so we come to feel more confident in using them. As we practice, so we gain a better understanding of what they mean, how they should sound and where we should use them.

Here are five techniques to help students practice using new words:

- **Whole-Class Call and Response.** Stand at the front of the classroom and say the word out loud. Students respond by repeating the word back to you. Develop by changing the pace at which you speak, by using the word in phrases and sentences and by calling it out phonetically.

- **Paired Call and Response.** As above expect this time students work in pairs. Initially, Student A is the caller and Student B the responder. They then swap over so that both have a go at each role.

- **Contrived Sentences.** Display a contrived sentence on the board. That is, one which contains the new word (or words) you want students to practice a number of times. Invite the class to speak the sentence out loud repeatedly – either as a whole class or in pairs.

- **Spot the Error.** Display five sentences on the board, each containing the new word. One of these should demonstrate incorrect usage. Ask students to speak all of the sentences out loud and to then identify which one contains the error.

- **Show Me an Error.** A reversal of the above. Students construct five sentences of their own, one of which must contain an incorrect usage. They then test these out on their partner, who must speak them aloud and spot the error.

Word Banks

16 Word banks break up the cognitive load for students. You can use them in writing activities and in speaking activities. They let students focus their attention on the act of writing or speaking, without having to divide their working memory between this and attempted recollection of keywords or phrases. As such, a word bank is a scaffold which can be withdrawn once the student has gained confidence – and practice – in using the keywords.

Here is an example of a word bank:

During a religious studies lesson focussing on religious festivals, the teacher provides students with the following word bank:

Festival	Easter	Diwali
Eid	Ritual	Tradition
Rules	Worship	Community
Prayer	Faith	Remembrance

This is used as a supplement during discussion activities in the first half of the lesson and during a writing activity towards the end of the lesson. In both cases, the word bank helps direct student thinking. It also lets students focus on speaking and writing about the topic, without having to divide their energy between that and recalling the keywords.

Sentence Starters

17 Sentence starters are another example of scaffolding. In this case, the teacher is providing students with a route into their writing. The sentence starters do a little bit of the work for the student, whose is then free to focus on what comes next.

Some students find starting writing difficult. This can be for a number of reasons, including:

- Uncertainty over how to begin

- Lack of confidence

- A perception that there are too many possibilities from which to select

- Feeling daunted by the sight of a blank piece of paper

- A belief that whatever they choose to do will be the wrong option

Sentence starters dispel all this ambiguity and uncertainty without doing too much of the work for the student. It is like the teacher saying: 'Here's how to start, now go ahead and show me what you can do.'

You can share sentence starters verbally with students, display them on the board, or provide laminated handouts containing common examples (to which students can return again and again).

Over time, you will hopefully see your students requiring less and less of this support. However, should you notice a student who continues to request sentence starters after an extended period of time, you may need to sit down and discuss with them why this is the case.

Model Sentences

18 Model sentences give students an example they can use to inform their own writing. They help students understand what success looks like and also act as a starting point for framing thoughts. One that can be internalised and re-used over time.

Of particular interest is the fact that different subjects require different modes of writing at different times. While there is considerable overlap, for example, between analytical writing in history and in English, there is nearly always significant variation in content and in the technical language or genre rules students are expected to use in different areas of the curriculum.

Model sentences can help students navigate between the different expectations they meet in different subjects or at different age groups. Here are some examples of how to use them:

- Provide students with examples of sentence types they will regularly need to use in a subject. For example, a history teacher might create a handout containing five model sentences students can imitate or borrow from to write about sources.

- Start a written activity by showing students a set of three model sentences relevant to the task. Talk students through how you constructed the sentences, why they are apt and how they connect together.

- Share an annotated set of model sentences. The annotations should give access to the thinking which has underpinned their construction. In doing this you help students to develop a metacognitive awareness of what makes a sentence good in a given context.

Genre Conventions

19 I mentioned in the last entry that different genres of writing have different rules. If students are writing a poem they do not write in the same way as when they write a book report. Similarly, if you read a newspaper you do not expect to find the written word being used in an identical manner to when you read a recipe.

Helping students understand genre conventions means getting the implicit rules of writing out into the open. This serves a number of purposes. First, it makes it easier for students to read and interpret within that genre. Second, it makes it easier for them to write in that genre and to assess their own efforts. Third, it helps them to understand the differences between different types of writing – even if the medium of expression (written words) is the same.

Here are five simple strategies for opening up genre conventions:

- Make a list of key genre rules and share this with students.

- Give students a checklist they can use to assess whether a text they are reading belongs to a certain genre – or whether what they are writing belongs to that genre.

- Annotate a piece of text to show how and why it conforms to a particular genre.

- Read a text out loud. As you go through, stop and narrate your thinking to students – that is, the comprehension strategies you are using to interpret the text and identify the genre to which it belongs.

- Use genre conventions incorrectly. For example, present a serious news story as a poem, or answer an exam question using local dialect. Then, discuss with students why this feels wrong and what it reveals about the correct genre conventions.

Writing Models

20 Point, evidence, explain. PEE for short. Maybe you were taught this paragraph-writing model at school – or learned how to use something similar.

The great benefit of a writing model is that it does some of the work for you. Setting out to write a new paragraph, you do not have to divide your attention between what you want to say and how you will try to say it. PEE has taken care of the second part for you. It has also given you a lens through which to think about the first part.

Over time, users of PEE internalise the model, making it their own. This tends to result in them writing effective paragraphs automatically. Or, at least, it will if they engage in sufficient practice.

What is true of PEE is true of writing models more generally. They help students out by doing a bit of work for them. They provide a sound structure on which students can hang their ideas.

You can apply some writing models across the curriculum – such as PEE – whereas others are age or subject-specific. Your use of them will vary depending on who and what you teach. However, in all cases they are a means through which to improve and develop the quality of student writing.

Structure Guidelines

21 If a writing model is a specific framework to which students must adhere, structure guidelines offer a looser set of rules students can follow to improve the quality of their work. We can illustrate the difference using our existing example of PEE:

Writing Model: PEE – You must create paragraphs which conform to this structure.

Structure Guidelines: You should ensure your story has a beginning, a middle and an end.

While the structure guidelines are in part similarly definitive (the story *should* have a beginning, a middle and an end), they are also much looser in definition. What constitutes a beginning, a middle and an end is not specified. Students have freedom and scope to experiment; to try things out.

The difference is thus one of degree.

Here are some further examples of structure guidelines you can adapt for the classes you teach:

- The first half of your essay should focus on analysis, the second half on evaluation.

- I want to know what you think at the start and at the end of your book report.

- Good answers will include examples which get increasingly specific.

- Your speech should include a selection of the rhetorical techniques we've looked at.

- Definitions need to come first, before interpretations.

Defining Purpose

22 Purpose gives direction. Direction helps us focus our energy. Energy is finite. If we can target our efforts as effectively as possible, then we are likely to make more efficient use of our energy.

When asking students to speak, listen, read or write, we can give them a clear purpose they can use to target their efforts and maximise the impact of what they do.

In some of the earlier entries we saw purpose being defined in the context of discussion. For example, Entry Nine, Interviewing, sees students being given a twin purpose – to hear the thoughts of their peers and to share their own thoughts. This is further circumscribed if specific questions are provided as the basis of the interviewing.

You can define purpose in any activity in which students are engaged. Giving this a specific literacy dimension helps remind students of the wider importance of what they are doing. Here are some examples of purpose being defined very tightly, in an effort to enhance students' literacy skills:

- I want you to write your answer as if the reader has no prior knowledge of the topic.

- I want you to use this essay as an opportunity to focus exclusively on implementing your target.

- The purpose of this discussion is to see if you can change your partner's mind.

- The purpose of this discussion is to practice using three of the keywords I've put on the board. You decide which three.

- When you're reading the source, I want you to think about how you could use it to disprove Smith's interpretation of the events of 1832.

Defining Success

23 Another way we can help students to effectively target their efforts is by defining what success looks like. This is applicable to all four elements of literacy. It gives students an understanding of what they are trying to achieve. They can then work towards this, checking their work as they go to see how closely it accords with the goal. Here are four examples of the technique, one for each element:

- Speaking. The teacher defines success as follows: During the discussion you need to share your argument with your partner three times. Each time you must improve your argument. By the end of the discussion, I want you to be ready to share a stronger, more persuasive argument than you had at the start.

- Listening. Success is defined as: You need to identify the three most important things the newsreader says. This might involve you changing your mind as you hear more of the report. At the end, you should be able to explain to us why you made your choices.

- Reading. The following is used to define success: When you've read the chapter, I want you to be able to tell me why you think Mr Darcy behaves like he does. You're explanation will need to reference the text.

- Writing. The teacher defines success like this: A good piece of work will include evidence of editing, lots of examples and a conclusion.

Notice how, in each case, and to varying degrees, the definition of success serves to target students' effort, causing them to act in specific and focused ways.

Exemplar Work

24 Exemplar work can be created by the teacher or can be work (anonymised or not) produced by students. In either case it acts as an exemplification of what students are trying to achieve in a given task.

So, for example, we might be working with students on a piece of written work. In which case, we present them with a piece of exemplar work we have written, designed to show them what they are working towards.

At this point, a few options are open to us. First, we can give out copies of the exemplar work and let students use these as an aid while they are writing. Second, we can give out copies of the exemplar work and use these as the basis of a discussion. Third, we can display the exemplar work on the board and talk students through different aspects of it.

These three options show the varying degree to which you can use exemplar work to unpick and illustrate the features of high-quality writing.

You can also use it in speaking tasks, although this is slightly more complicated. It requires the creation of audio or video files which capture high-quality speaking being demonstrated by the teacher or a student. While this can take a little more time and effort than the creation of exemplar written work, the same benefits can be derived.

And, as an alternative, you might choose to use clips from YouTube of famous speakers exemplifying high-quality speech in different contexts.

Annotated Exemplar Work

25 A particularly powerful and oft overlooked way of using exemplar work sees the teacher providing it to students complete with annotations. These annotations focus not on what can be seen in the text – the writing itself – but on the thinking and decision-making which has given rise to the writing.

Using exemplar work in this way means helping students to think critically about their own thought processes and the decisions in which they engage when producing a piece of writing.

Here is an example of the technique in action:

In a Year 6 science lesson the teacher hands out an exemplar report of an experiment. The same experiment students have just completed and which they are now going to begin writing up.

The exemplar work was written by the teacher. They wrote it on three pieces of A5 paper, which they then stuck to three pieces of A4 paper. This gave them space around the edge in which they could annotate their work.

The teacher leads the class in analysing and discussing both the original work and the annotations. Through this process, students gain access to what good work looks like, and to the thinking and decision-making underpinning the production of high-quality writing. This leaves them in a much stronger position to start their write-up compared to if they had gone into it cold.

Goldfish Bowl

26 As noted, it is harder to use exemplar work with speaking and listening. This reflects the ephemeral nature of speech, contrasted with the permanent (or semi-permanent) nature of writing.

One way in which you can 'annotate' exemplar speaking and listening is through the goldfish bowl activity. It can take a few attempts to get right, but is usually worth the effort. Here's how it works:

Identify a pair of students (A & B) who consistently demonstrate excellent speaking and listening skills. Move the furniture to the side of the room. Place a pair of chairs in the middle of the floor and invite Students A and B to sit there. Next, ask the rest of the class to arrange their chairs in a circle around them.

Explain what is going to happen: Students A and B are going to discuss a topic or a series of questions and you are going to stop them at certain points. You will then outline why what the students are doing is good, and talk about some of the thought processes underpinning their actions.

The activity goes ahead, you make as many interventions as you feel appropriate and, if relevant, you have a student scribing summaries of your comments on the board for the class to see (and later use).

This activity does rely on you having two confident, skilled students who are happy to be the model for the rest of the class. However, done well, it can provide a huge amount of insight in a short period of time, supercharging the subsequent rate of improvement in students' speaking and listening.

Narrated Marking

27 Some apps and learning platforms now let you record your voice and attach it to an electronic copy of a student's work. For example, you set your class an essay, they complete it using their computers, email you a copy, which you then read and mark verbally. You return the essay to your students, with the audio file attached for them to listen to.

This has obvious benefits as well as barriers to entry (primarily the fact that all students need to be on board with the technology).

When it comes to writing, narrated marking of this type can be really valuable. The student receives information which is easier for the teacher to convey – and potentially easier for them to process – than if it were done in written form. The student can simultaneously listen to the feedback and look at their essay – as opposed to switching between reading the teacher's comments and reading their own writing.

I don't believe such technology will ever replace written feedback – but it does offer an interesting and useful alternative. One you might like to explore and try out, with a specific focus on the development of literacy.

Modelling Thought Processes

28 In a number of the entries thus far I have drawn out or alluded to the importance of helping students gain access to the thought processes underpinning effective speaking, listening, reading and writing. We can group all of this together under a single category, namely, the modelling of thought processes.

As teachers, when we do this, we give students access to our expertise – as expert speakers, listeners, readers and writers. In so doing, we help students understand what they need to do to become more expert, how they can change their thinking, and, also, we cause them to reflect on why their present thinking is leading to certain results.

Here are four examples, in addition to those already included as part of other entries, of how you can model literacy thought processes for your students:

- Read a piece of text aloud. As you do, stop at opportune moments and describe the thinking in which you are engaged while you are reading.

- Play a video or audio clip to the class. As you are all listening, pause the clip at certain points and talk through the thinking which is underpinning your listening.

- Invite students to come up with questions they want to ask you connected to the current topic. Let them pose some of these questions to you. As you answer, take time to also talk about how you are answering and the thinking which is preceding your verbalisation.

- Use screen capturing to record yourself writing two or three paragraphs on Microsoft Word. Play the video to your class and talk them through the thinking which underpinned what you did.

Six Ways to Start a Sentence

29 This is a common technique through which to help students vary their sentences and thus improve the quality of their writing. The six ways are:

I. **The Subject.** <u>The woman</u> sashayed across the road.

II. **A Participle.** <u>Running</u> in the woods, he saw it.

III. **A Conjunction.** <u>As</u> she climbed on board, she thought of home.

IV. **An Adverb.** <u>Happily</u> he didn't mean it.

V. **An Adjective.** <u>Large</u> and muscular, this looked like a well-fed animal.

VI. **A Phrase.** <u>Furious at the world and at himself</u>, he decided to buy an ice-cream.

This list is not exhaustive, nor is it the only combination of six ways to start a sentence. But it does provide students with a helpful tool. You can remind them of it on a regular basis, or even hand out copies for them to stick in their books.

As an aside, it is worth noting that the principle can be adapted for specific subjects. For example, you might decide to come up with 'Six Ways to Start a Sentence in Geography.'

Defining the Audience

30 I know who you are. At least, I think I do. As I write this book, I do so on the assumption that you, the reader, is likely to be an education professional. That you have an existing knowledge and understanding of teaching and learning, that literacy development is a priority for you (or at least an interest), and that you are familiar with key concepts and ideas connected to education.

While I might not be right about this in all cases, it provides me with a reasonable and realistic model from which to work.

Having defined my audience, in my own mind, I am then in a position to target my writing towards that audience. Consider, for example, how the book might differ if it was aimed at parents or students.

You can help students improve their writing and speaking by demonstrating the importance of defining an audience. A fun way to do this is by presenting them with texts which are far too easy for them and acting like you don't see the problem.

So, for example, a Year 7 teacher might use an extract from a book aimed at 6 year-olds. They would pretend to take this seriously, pressing students to analyse sentences such as 'Spot has found his bowl,' before revealing the real purpose of the activity – to encourage students to think critically about who they are writing for and why knowing your audience can have major benefits when it comes to writing and speaking.

Keyword Quotas

31 This activity is a variation of Word Banks (see Entry Sixteen). Here is an example of it being used in a GCSE sociology lesson:

Education	Gender	Ethnicity	Identity
Inequality	Culture	Norms	Values
Roles	Status	Family	Class
Socialisation	Agency	Evidence	Research

Task: You have ten minutes to write an introduction to the study of sociology for new students. Your minimum keyword quota is eight. It's up to you if you want to use more than eight keywords. No lists and no bullet points allowed!

We are using a word bank here for the same reasons as outlined earlier. We have moved things on a step by setting a keyword quota. That is, a minimum number of keywords students must include in their writing. We have further increased the level of challenge by injecting some ambiguity as to whether or not to use more than eight keywords and by outlawing lists and bullet points.

Overall, the activity focuses students' attention on using the keywords and thinking about how their writing must be shaped around these. You can adapt the approach for use across the curriculum. In so doing, play around with the size of the word bank, the size of the quota and the use of additional caveats. See what different results this can engender.

Keyword Mindmaps

32 A mindmap is a way of visually rendering our existing thoughts and knowledge about a given topic. Students can use mindmaps as a way to make writing easier, and as a tool to support speaking and listening.

In the first case, let us imagine that we have a class of students and that we want them to write something on the topic of Greek myths. To begin, we ask them to each create a mindmap with the keyword (or phrase) 'Greek myths' at the centre. We give five minutes for this and then encourage students to move around the room and share their mindmaps with their peers, so that they can add to and develop their own.

Next, we explain what we would like students to write about. For example, we might ask them to write a piece explaining what Greek myths are, why we still read them today and what their personal favourite is and why.

Students are in a strong position to produce a detailed, high-quality piece of work. They have in front of them a fully developed mindmap visualising their thoughts and knowledge about Greek myths. They can use this to structure their writing and, of course, it acts as an extension of working memory, meaning they can focus most of their attention on saying what they want to say, without having to devote thinking power to recollection and recall.

Now, consider a similar activity, but one in which the writing task is swapped for a discussion task. Students continue to derive great benefit from the mindmap; it becomes a supporting tool for their discussions in the same way as it was for their writing.

Verbal Feedback

33 Feedback has been shown time and again to be one of the most effective teaching and learning interventions. Here are four examples of how to use verbal feedback to help students improve their literacy:

- **Reading.** Identify two or three of the weakest readers in your class. While they are reading, give them feedback on their comprehension strategies. That is, the strategies they are using to make sense of the text. This could be in response to them reading aloud, or in response to the answers they give to questions you pose about the text they are reading.

- **Writing.** While students are engaged in a writing task, circulate through the room. Identify two or three students who will most benefits from your feedback. Read their work and give them a specific target they can swiftly implement. Leave them to do this and return 2-3 minutes later to discuss the impact it has had.

- **Speaking.** During discussion activities, circulate through the room listening to student conversations. When you hear a discussion which isn't sufficiently in-depth, detailed or analytical, give students a highly specific question to discuss, derived from the general topic, but which will help them to retrain their focus. As with the writing example, return shortly after to observe (and discuss) the results.

- **Listening.** Observe how students respond to each other during discussions. If you identify a discussion in which students are simply waiting to speak, instead of responding to what has been said, intervene by offering verbal feedback. Model the difference between waiting to speak and responding to what you have heard. Let students restart their conversations and listen in to check whether your feedback has been take on board.

Editing Techniques

34 Speech is instantly editable. For example, we might rephrase our thoughts having heard ourselves speak, or we might change our position based on what our friend says to us. It takes a little longer to edit writing. And some students are reluctant to do this at all. Teaching editing techniques is one way to make the process easier and more accessible. Here are three examples:

- **Spelling, Punctuation, Sense.** Ask students to edit their work by first examining the spelling, then examining the punctuation, before finally examining whether it makes sense and conveys what they wanted it to convey. This editing technique does not always result in students making changes, but it does cause them to look more carefully at what they have written. It is particularly good for getting students to pick up on careless mistakes.

- **Weakest Paragraph.** Ask students to look back through their work and to pick out the weakest paragraph they have written. It is up to you whether you define what weakest means in this sense, or whether you leave it open for students to interpret. Once the weakest paragraph has been identified, students should rewrite it. In longer pieces of work you might ask them to identify the weakest section rather than just a single paragraph.

- **Choose Three Things.** This technique sees you asking students to choose three things about their work to change. You can specify what type of things these can be, or leave it open. Either way, the onus is on the student to make three edits which enhance the quality of their final piece.

Literacy Checklists

35 Checklists help us overcome the limitations of working memory. They also let us take advantage of knowledge gained in the past. You can develop your own literacy checklists and share these with students. They can then practice using them before, over time, internalising them. The behaviour captured by the checklists then becomes automatic.

One of the editing techniques in the last entry was a checklist: Spelling, Punctuation, Sense. Here are some others you might like to use:

- **Reading.** (i) Author, Audience, Purpose, Form. The student asks themselves who the author is, who they are writing for, why they are writing and what form that writing takes. (ii) What do I know? What don't I know? What do I need to find out? The student identifies what they already know about the text or topic, what gaps in their knowledge they are aware of and, as a result, what they need to focus on finding out.

- **Writing.** (i) Plan, Write, Check. The student is reminded of the importance of planning and checking, with these bookending the act of writing. The checklist can be applied to a whole piece but also to individual sections and paragraphs.

- **Speaking.** (i) Ethos, Logos, Pathos. This is the set of appeals identified by ancient rhetoricians. Ethos is the appeal to ethics and personal character, logos to logic and reason, and pathos to emotions and feelings.

- **Listening.** (i) Listen, Clarify, Summarise. The student listens to their interlocutor, uses questions to clarify what is being said and then summarises this to check they have correctly understood.

Self-Assessment

36 If you can make accurate judgements about your work, then you are in a position to make positive changes. If you can't make accurate judgements – if your judgements are consistently inaccurate – then it becomes much harder to be certain whether what you are doing is right.

If students can make accurate judgements about the work they do connected to literacy – be that reading, writing, speaking or listening – then they are in a better position to identify what they need to do next, why they need to do it and what impact they hope to have by making changes.

You can improve students' ability to self-assess in a number of ways. These include:

- Providing specific, literacy-focussed success criteria. For example, covering how to read a given text or how to contribute to a discussion. See also Entry Twenty Three.

- Providing students with a set of categories through which to look at their work. For example, when it comes to writing the categories might be: form, style, language, coherence, readability.

- Training students in how to self-assess. This treats it as skill which needs to be learned through practice.

- Modelling self-assessment. For example, by critiquing the speaking and listening you engaged in at a recent meeting.

- Creating examples of good, bad and indifferent self-assessment and giving students time to analyse and contrast these.

Focussed Practice

37 Practice makes perfect. But passive or inattentive practice is no guarantee of good results. Focussed practice, in which attention is focussed on repeating a specific act, is more likely to bring good results. This is because we are actively engaged with what we are doing – attending to it as it happens.

Here are examples of focussed practice for each element of literacy:

- **Reading.** The teacher provides a series of five short texts. Students read each one in turn and have to answer the same set of questions, apply the same comprehension strategy, or identify the three key points in each.

- **Writing.** The teacher sets a series of related questions around the same topic. They provide a set of success criteria and ask students to answer each question in turn by creating answers of similar length. A metacognitive element is brought in by the teacher pausing the activity after each answer is completed and asking students to review what they have done and what they could change in their next effort.

- **Speaking.** The teacher sets up a discussion activity in which students have repeated opportunities to articulate their ideas. Examples include Triads (Entry Four) and Interviewing (Entry Nine).

- **Listening.** The teacher plays students a sequence of audio/visual clips in which different individuals talk about the same event from different perspectives. Students are given a checklist which they apply on each occasion. When all the clips have been heard, students compare their notes with a partner and review the results of their listening.

Active Repetition with Targets

38 This is a variation on the theme introduced in the previous entry. Active repetition with targets sees students practising a specific element of literacy, with this practice driven by a target they are seeking to implement.

For example, we might set our class an exam-style question, take in the work they produce, mark it and then return it to them with targets written on. Next lesson, we set up an activity in which students have to complete three successive exam-style questions identical in form to the first one they attempted. The difference, however, is that they must try to implement their targets on each occasion.

While such tasks can be boring for students, the benefits outweigh any tedium – but only up to a point. If you ask them to do too much repetition, their focus will wane. This scuppers the activity because effort ceases to be targeted. Instead, students start going through the motions. They stop thinking about what their targets mean and how they are trying to implement them. The activity becomes procedural rather than meaningful. Finding the right amount of repetition requires a little trial and error – and it will differ from class to class.

Reading Techniques

39 Reading is a hard skill for the non-literacy specialist to develop. This is partly because of its invisibility and also because of the lack of certainty over whether developments have taken place in the student's mind. These can't be directly accessed. Instead, they have to be accessed indirectly through questioning, listening, observation or reading the work the student produces.

Nonetheless, there is still much we can do to support our students. This includes teaching reading techniques such as the following:

- **Skimming.** This is where we skim the text looking for main features, standout words and phrases, headings, subheadings and other such elements. It helps us to gain the gist of what has been written without fully comprehending it.

- **Scanning.** Here we scan sentences, paragraphs and pages in search of specific pieces of information. Scanning also covers images and illustrations. It allows for a higher level of comprehension than skimming but not full comprehension of a text.

- **Intensive Reading.** This requires much more time than skimming and scanning but results in a far fuller understanding of a text. Intensive reading is most effective when the student has a clear purpose in mind. For example, to understand how the original write-up of a psychological study compares to the summary found in a textbook.

- **Extensive Reading.** Here students read a variety of texts connected to the topic. By doing this they build up a clearer picture of the topic predicated, at least in part, on a more developed understanding of how separate elements relate and interconnect.

When promoting reading techniques the first step is to make students aware of the different options. The second step is to model examples by narrating the thought processes in which you engage when using the different techniques.

Reading for Questions

40 Another way we can help students to read more effectively is by providing them with a set of questions they need to answer via their reading. The questions provide a clear purpose. Students assimilate the text knowing that they are trying to find answers to the questions you've posed.

Here is an example:

Task: Read the speech by Amartya Sen. As you do, identify information which can help you answer the following questions:

1) How might Sen characterise the economics profession?

2) What values do you think underpin Sen's approach to economics?

3) Is there sufficient evidence in the speech to support the main argument?

If students are reading to answer questions, you are in a position to easily and effectively scaffold the work for them. Continuing with our example, we might provide students who are struggling with the following clues:

- Look at paragraphs 3, 4 and 6 for help with the first question.

- You could answer Question 2 by comparing the introduction and the conclusion.

- Evidence is usually contained in the main body of a speech. This will help you to answer question 3.

This makes life easier for them, overcoming their present difficulties with reading at this level, but not so easy that they don't have to work hard. It reflects the central premise of good scaffolding – give the least amount of help first.

Reading and Note-Taking

41 As students progress through school, so are they increasingly expected to make notes. Reading becomes a two-step process. You must read in order to comprehend. And you must make notes to capture that understanding.

We can easily make the false assumption that students automatically know how to make good notes, or that someone else will have taught them what to do. This is often not the case. Often they do not know how to make good notes and will never have been formally taught how to do it. Taking a little bit of time to rectify this can have positive results.

Here are three note-taking strategies you can teach your students:

- **Cornell Method.** Take a sheet of A4 paper. Draw a vertical line which divides the page into one third (to the left) and two thirds (to the right). Stop when you are about 75% down the page. Draw a horizontal line across the width of the page at the point where the vertical line stops. The smaller left-hand column is for keywords and questions. The larger right-hand section is for notes connected to these. The bottom section is for an overall summary.

- **Visual Methods.** These include graphic organisers such as mindmaps, tables, diagrams and flow-charts. Some students find the presentation of information in this format to be more conducive to memory and understanding than other methods.

- **Symbols and Abbreviations.** Developing a system of symbols and abbreviations can aid recall and speed up the process of note-taking. Colour can be introduced as an additional element. For example, a student making notes for their psychology class might decide to use colour and symbol combinations to denote psychodynamic studies, behaviourist studies and cognitivist studies.

Decoding Texts – Tips and Techniques

42 As expert readers we understand there are many ways to decode texts. We frequently use a variety of methods to do this, usually without having to think actively about the process. Here are a range of decoding tips and techniques you can share with students, making it easier for them to decode new texts they encounter:

- **Look for clues.** These are anything which give you an insight into what the text is saying, including highlighted words, repeated phrases, quotes and so forth.

- **Use subheadings and similar.** Structural elements of a text signpost things the author thinks matter or deems worthy of inclusion.

- **Interpret through images and diagrams.** Visual information is often used to supplement written information. It gives the reader another way through which to access and check meaning.

- **Identify themes.** Themes are the guiding motifs which animate a text. Identifying these means you understand the organising principles the author is using to order their thoughts.

- **Search for keywords.** Keywords often signal technical or specialist language. They can also indicate where the most relevant information is within a text.

- **Question the author.** Asking questions of the author in your mind while you read helps maintain a critical perspective and avoids taking what the author is saying for granted.

- **Ask 'why?'** Why is this here? Why has this been included? Why write this and not that? Questions of this type help a reader to interrogate a text as they go.

Dictionaries and Thesauruses

43 Dictionaries and thesauruses are tools which help students to improve their literacy. This is an obvious fact. One I know you'll be familiar with but one some of your students might not always accept so readily. Here are four techniques for increasing use of the tools in lessons:

- **Model using a dictionary and/or thesaurus.** Can you be sure all your students know how to use a dictionary and thesaurus effectively? If not, modelling will unobtrusively show them how to do it. In addition, by modelling the process you give it credibility in students' eyes.

- **Set dictionary challenges.** Divide the class into teams and set a series of questions students have to use the dictionary to solve. For example: What word beginning with 'A' means friendly and easy-going? Or: How many different meanings does the word 'how' have?

- **Appoint dictionary and/or thesaurus champions.** These students look up words on behalf of the whole class and then report back. They also help students who are stuck or who are struggling to use their dictionaries or thesauruses.

- **Play 'Thesaurus Top Ten.'** Display a list of ten words on the board. Explain that students must work in pairs and that they need to create a list of ten synonyms, one for each word, using a thesaurus. Indicate that this is a game – the first team to finish wins – and that in the event of a tie the most creative list will be the winning one.

Dividing Up Writing

44 When faced with a writing task, some students can disengage for the simple reason that it seems like too much to do. They feel overwhelmed, uncertain where to begin or what they can do to be successful, and so they withdraw altogether.

For these students, it is crucial to identify a way to make writing easier. To help them access the work more effectively than would otherwise be the case. Perhaps the best method is to teach them how to divide up writing. Many students do this intuitively but, if you don't know how to do it, finding out can be a revelation.

Dividing up writing means deciding before you begin what different sections you will include, along with a rough estimate of how big these sections will be. This means you no longer have to write an extended piece. Instead, you only have to write a series of shorter pieces, all of which connect together.

Consider this book as an example. I did not sit down to write it and think, 'I must write thirteen thousand words.' Instead, I sat down and thought, 'What fifty separate entries can I write, connected to the main topic, and hopefully getting a fairly even split between the different areas of literacy?' I then worked my way through, writing each entry in turn.

There is no secret to dividing up writing. It's one of the simplest tricks in the book. But if a student doesn't know about it then they are at a big disadvantage compared to their peers.

Planning Techniques

45 The last entry was an example of a planning technique. We divide writing up before we start, making the act of writing easier as a result. Here are five more planning techniques you can share with students:

- **Write your conclusion first.** This can be a helpful way to get your ideas clear in your own mind. Having written your conclusion – and perhaps rewritten, refined or edited it – you can go about the task of writing with a clear idea of what you are working towards. And therefore what needs to be included and what should be omitted.

- **Delineate your paragraphs.** Decide how many paragraphs you will write and then decide what the purpose of each paragraph will be. Having done this, you have a clear structure on which to place the 'flesh' of your writing.

- **Select three main points.** Decide on the three main points you want to make in your writing and then put them in order of importance. Write about each one in turn, ticking off the points as you go.

- **Beginning, middle, end.** This plan can be used for non-fiction as well as for fiction writing. Viewing an essay, report or other piece of work through a narrative lens means seeing it as having a narrative structure.

- **Circle the clock.** Draw a circle. Make a list of the key points you want to cover in your writing. Order these from most to least important. Write the points around the circle, starting with the most important at '12 O'clock'. As you create your written work, cross out each point in turn until you've circled the clock. You don't have to include twelve separate points. For example, you could have four points – at 12, 3, 6 and 9 O'clock.

Thinking Maps

46 Thinking maps are a way to visualise different cognitive processes. Google 'thinking maps' and, on the image search, you will find a host of ready-made maps students can use to help them with their literacy. For example, maps are available covering: describing, analysing, cause and effect, analogies, classifying, evaluation and more besides.

You can share these maps with students, show them how to use them, and then encourage their use within discussion, reading and writing activities.

For example, you might use a classifying map as the basis for a student discussion around the question: 'Are there different types of justice?' The map helps students to speak and listen more effectively. It also provides a nice way for them to capture their ideas.

Another example would be a reading task in which students use a cause and effect map to distil information from a text. For example, we might give them a newspaper article about a recent election and ask them to use the map to identify what the article says about the causes and effects of the result.

Plenty of thinking maps are available for free online. Have a look and see which ones work for you and your students. And don't forget that what is out there has been made by fellow teachers – you can adapt and modify what you find. Or come up with your own entirely.

Whole-Class Bounce

47 When we pose a question to the class we often fall into the trap of taking an answer from a student, commenting on this, posing a second question, taking a second answer, commenting on this, and so on. We create a situation in which the focus goes: Teacher – Student – Teacher – Student – Teacher – Student.

There is nothing wrong with this per se. But what it does mean is that for the majority of the discussion the majority of the class are listening without being active participants. Now, sometimes that is fine, necessary and welcome. But, if done all the time, it can lead to passivity and a sense that all you need to do is sit there and *look* like your listening.

An alternative is whole-class bounce. It works as follows.

Teacher: Is nuclear energy the best way to replace fossil fuels? Thirty seconds, discuss with your partner.

30 second pass.

Teacher: Monica, what came up in your discussion?

Monica: Well, we said that nuclear has a lot of benefits but that the carbon footprint for building a plant is pretty high, so do you take that into account as well?

Teacher: Thank you, Monica. Thirty seconds, talk to your partner: Should we include the carbon cost of creating a nuclear power plant when we think about nuclear energy?

Notice that the teacher invites all students to discuss, then takes an answer which they bounce back to the whole class through a related question which moves the discussion on. The method can be repeated 3, 4 or 5 times to develop a significant discussion. In so doing, all students have a series of opportunities to speak and listen – guaranteeing their active involvement.

Distancing

48 Consider these two question formations:

A) What might democracy be?

B) What might democracy be? What might a person from another country think about this question? What about somebody from the nineteenth century?

Question A asks the student for their thoughts. Question B asks the student to think about what somebody else might think. This is distancing. The student is distanced from the subject of the question. Instead of asking them to share their views on the question, we ask them to put those to one side and think from a different perspective.

Using this technique has at least two benefits:

First, it is a good way to elicit answers from students who lack confidence or do not feel comfortable sharing their views. The distance created neutralises the fear of failure some students have – or the sense they might possess that what they think isn't worth sharing.

Second, it encourages students who are very comfortable articulating and sharing their own thoughts to take a step back and look at topics from a different perspective. This can be particularly helpful if we have students who are happy to speak but not to listen. The act of thinking from another's perspective promotes the wider importance of listening to what others think and say.

Modelling Great Literacy

49 Our penultimate idea is a familiar one: taking advantage of the power of modelling. Students observe what we do. They imitate our actions, internalise the behaviour they see, and use it as a guide to what is appropriate and what is not.

When it comes to literacy, modelling great reading, writing, speaking and listening means giving students an exemplar from which to borrow, copy and develop their own ideas. If you consistently model great literacy in your classroom, then you are consistently giving students access to your expertise as a reader, writer, speaker and listener.

One area of modelling which is sometimes overlooked is the modelling of mistake-making and responding to mistakes. When it comes to literacy, we all make mistakes, get things wrong and engage in trial and error. Modelling this for your students means showing them how to deal positively with mistakes.

For example, we might correct ourselves while we are speaking and briefly draw attention to what we have done and why we've done it. Or, we might share the first draft of something we wrote with students, along with the second and third drafts which followed. Doing things like this on a regular basis normalises mistake-making and helps students to see it as a part of learning; something we can learn from, rather than something which must be avoided at all costs.

Websites and Resources

50 To conclude our journey through improving literacy across the curriculum, here are a selection of websites offering materials, support and resources you can use to further develop your practice:

- literacytrust.org.uk – The National Literacy Trust

- ukla.org – The UK Literacy Association

- literacyshed.com – UK-Based Teacher-Created Website

- ncte.org/ncle – The National Center for Literacy Education (US)

- clpe.org.uk – Centre for Literacy in Primary Education – UK Charity

- unesco.org/literacy – United Nations Educational, Scientific and Cultural Organisation

- teachingideas.co.uk/subjects/English – Selection of Online Resources

- learningspy.co.uk/ - Teaching Blog with a Literacy Focus

- geoffbarton.co.uk/ - Headteacher and Author's Website with Lots of Teaching Resources

And with that our journey comes to an end. I hope you've found the book useful and that some of the ideas I've outlined can help your students to make great progress in their reading, writing, speaking and listening. As ever, trial and error is the best approach to take. Try things out, see what works, and make changes until you settle on something that fits you and your students. I'm sure you'll produce some great results.

A Brief Request

If you have found this book useful I would be delighted if you could leave a review on Amazon to let others know.

If you have any thoughts or comments, or if you have an idea for a new book in the series you would like me to write, please don't hesitate to get in touch at mike@mikegershon.com.

Finally, don't forget that you can download all my teaching and learning resources for **FREE** at www.mikegershon.com and www.gershongrowthmindsets.com

Printed in Great Britain
by Amazon